The Meditative Approach to Philosophy

Dennis E. Bradford, Ph.D.

Copyright

Legal disclaimer

Contents

Introduction

Warning: Please do not attach yourself to the following ideas.

If, as I argue in The 7 Steps to Mastery, the common judgment that humans beings are separate selves is false, then any categorization of separate selves such as the one that follows is fatuous. It is not separate selves who are enlightened (realized) or not; rather, it is actions that are enlightened or not. Nevertheless, considering bad ideas can be helpful and discarding them for appropriate reasons is intellectual progress.

Furthermore, as Descartes (the father of modern western philosophy) noted, "there is nothing about which there is not some dispute."[1] Because they might be false, it's dangerous to attach to any ideas.

So please only use the following ideas to give yourself some initial traction and then discard them.

Philosophy

Mastery requires disciplined, focused, persistent training of the right kind. Only a fool would think, for example, that someone could become a master (world-class) athlete or a master (great) musician without years of the right kind of practice. Merely trying to master something never works; mastery is beyond trying. It requires sustained, wholehearted commitment. **Masters are made, not born.**

Philosophy is a serious attempt to master life. Etymologically, a philosopher is a lover of wisdom. Since to be wise is to live well, a philosopher is someone who lives well or seriously seeks to live well. A genuine philosopher is wholeheartedly committed to mastering life.

It is not obvious how to live well. Unlike aging, living well is not something that happens automatically. Furthermore, unlike knowing that, for example, $1 + 1 = 2$ or that red is a color, it isn't easy to understand what it means to live well; there are rational disagreements about the nature of wisdom. The necessary propaedeutics to philosophy are the uncomfortable admission of ignorance about what to do to live well and the decision that such ignorance is intolerable.

There are three kinds of people who never become philosophers:

(i) Those who believe that they already have all the answers to life's most important questions never become philosophers; why should they seek for something they believe they have? These people are "fanatics." To be a fanatic is to live with unquestioned attachment to a view. Being a fanatic is the opposite of being a philosopher.

(ii) Those who believe that there are no answers, that nobody ever lives well, also never become philosophers; why should they seek for something they believe doesn't exist? These people are also fanatics; they suffer from an unquestioned attachment to negativity or pessimism.

(iii) Those who are too afraid of the consequences of admitting the necessity of seeking never become philosophers; why should they endure the trauma of learning about various understandings of what it means to live well and seeking how to evaluate them when they can live easier lives of incessant (though ultimately unsatisfying) distractions? These people are trapped by fear. People who live in any of these three ways unnecessarily condemn themselves to living poorly.

People become philosophers only reluctantly, only when they exhaust easier options. Even just beginning to think seriously, to question all one's familiar judgments, is disorienting and disturbing. Every genuine philosopher goes through a baptism of fire.

Here are three classic examples:

5

The Meditative Approach to Philosophy

The Buddha, who was born a prince, gave up his family and privileged social position to become an impoverished seeker and nearly died in the process.

Plato compared the initial mental numbing of beginning to do philosophy to having one's body numbed by a torpedo ray.[2] He understood this because he lived it.

Descartes compared the disturbing initial disorientation caused by beginning to search for fundamental understanding to having fallen into a deep whirlpool and being unable either to touch a foot to the bottom or to swim to the top of the water.[3]

What all philosophers share is that they live examined lives. Philosophers seriously question life. Philosophers are people who are determined to live well or to die attempting to live well. It's not that a seeker endures the initial uncertainty because of some perverse enjoyment; it's that a serious seeker is wholeheartedly committed to living well and believes that the only way to give oneself a chance to live well is to lead an examined life. Living an examined life is not the same as living well; **the purpose of philosophy is to live well**, not to spend one's life merely seeking how to live well. If life is worth living, and it is, it is worth living well. Living well requires living an examined life. As Plato put it, "the unexamined life is not worth living."[4]

Though vague and abstract, this provides an initially useful categorization of human beings. A human being is either a nonphilosopher or a philosopher. A philosopher is either as-yet-unsuccessful or successful (living well). Imagine two vertical lines on a sheet of paper; label the columns from left to right '1', '2', and '3.'   Everyone is either in category 1 (nonphilosopher), category 2 (as-yet-unsuccessful philosopher) or category 3 (successful philosopher, sage). The dream of philosophers is to live well, to attain category 3. Sages, the greatest lovers, naturally encourage others to follow the way to wisdom. The purpose of life is to live as well as possible.

Here's a concrete analogy that may help:

Imagine finding yourself on an island surrounded by a dangerous sea. For a while, like a child playing in a toxic waste dump, you try to enjoy yourself, until you realize that there's no water or food on the island. You don't want to do nothing and die.

Deciding to do whatever it takes to keep alive, you build a raft, launch it, and begin paddling. Even though you do not know where you are going, you realize that you cannot stay where you are and, so, must change your location. Realizing that you need to change is extremely uncomfortable. You think you see some smoke in the distance and head toward it.

Eventually, you beach your raft on the mainland, satisfy your thirst and hunger, and build your own fire so that others still on the island or at sea may be able to see from the smoke of your fire which direction to go.

Permit me two additional points about this analogy.

First, notice that, once you get to the mainland, since your raft will have become useless, you'll naturally discard it. Think of the raft as being made of words and concepts—useful but ultimately eliminable. Getting attached to the raft is foolish.

The Meditative Approach to Philosophy

Second, completing a journey is accomplishing something, gaining a different location. This is where the analogy breaks down. A successful philosopher, a "sage", lives "without-thinking." Attaining "without-thinking" is not an accomplishment; rather, it's an uncovering, a letting go of both thinking and not-thinking. A sage "realizes" what was present all along. There's nothing to be accomplished. **There's nothing to be gained.**

Common misunderstandings about philosophy abound. I use 'philosopher' so that many folks not even associated with Western academic philosophy are, nevertheless, philosophers. There isn't just one way of living an examined life; there are many. A novelist could be a philosopher, as could a painter or a poet or a scientist or a historian or a monk/nun or a carpenter or a farmer or a merchant and so on.

Don't confuse studying philosophy in a classroom with being a philosopher. Don't confuse thinking about living well with living well. Philosophy is an academic discipline, but it's not merely that. Though it is possible to study philosophy, it is not possible to become a sage merely by thinking about it. Philosophy is a way of life. It is useless unless practiced, unless improvements in understanding show themselves in behavior.

It's a bit like this: it is possible to study the physiology of exercise and to understand a lot about it in the classroom, but, by itself, that understanding is useless in terms of making you stronger or fitter. To benefit from your study, you must actually exercise, in other words, use your understanding. Some understanding is important if you want to exercise—without it, you'd have no idea what to do. If, though, you spend all your time improving your understanding and never exercising, you'll never become stronger or fitter. Merely understanding is not doing. Similarly, unless you practice philosophy, you will never become wise. This explains why it sometimes happens that even a professor of philosophy is not a philosopher. (My guess is that most philosophy professors are not sages, and many are not even genuine philosophers.)

In fact, some sages have never studied philosophy in a classroom. This must be true, because who would have taught the first sage? Furthermore, many philosophers insist that too much classroom work is actually detrimental to success. Some understanding is critically important if you want to live well—without it, you'd have no idea what to do. If, though, you spend all your time improving your (conceptual) understanding and never actually practicing, you'll never live better.

So please don't confuse thinking well with living well. Some good thinking is necessary to living well, but it is not necessary to become a master thinker in order to live well and becoming a master thinker is detrimental to living well if it detracts from practicing philosophy. Like the raft in the analogy, thinking well (conceptually) is not intrinsically valuable; it is an ultimately dispensable means to the end of living well.

Why not, then, just live well and skip all the hard, fundamental thinking? It's because without thinking we would have no idea what to do. The values we adopt determine how we live, and every coherent set of values is grounded upon an understanding of reality. It is impossible to live without choosing. An evaluation is the essence of every choice, and every choice occurs within a context, within a certain understanding of reality. It is therefore important to examine the

The Meditative Approach to Philosophy

nature of values and understanding and reality. **Reality, understanding, and value are the fundamental ideas.**

Aren't all people naturally philosophers? No. However, all normal people, especially when they are children, do occasionally wonder, do occasionally examine life.

For a nonphilosophic adult, however, this usually only occurs seriously when there is a crisis that calls into question the value of how that person lives. For example, if a nonphilosophic man invests twenty years in raising a family and abruptly his wife and all their children are killed in a disaster, he's likely to take a step back to examine seriously the value of what he has been doing. In fact, if he doesn't commit suicide, such a traumatic event might prompt that man to begin to lead an examined life.

The difference between someone who is an occasional philosopher (in 1) and someone who is a philosopher (in 2) is deliberate commitment, a major decision to adopt the life of philosophy and then regularly examining life without waiting for inevitable crises as motivation for additional examination. Why wait until your well runs dry to begin digging a new one? Again there's an analogy to physical exercise. Distinguish pervasive unsatisfactoriness from pain; unlike pervasive unsatisfactoriness, pain is an inevitable part of life. Often, though, you can choose how you experience it.

You can, for example, choose to avoid the pain of exercise and the discomfort of disciplining your other physical habits such as diet, drug use, and sleep patterns, and, so, to increase your chances of experiencing the pain of the common lifestyle diseases of our age such as heart disease, stroke, cancer, and diabetes, or you can choose the pain and inconvenience of an appropriate disciplined path and, so, to increase your chances of experiencing freedom from the pain of such diseases.

Also, notice that there's no guarantee that rational physical habits will eliminate the chances of your enduring the pain of those diseases; similarly, there's no guarantee that becoming a philosopher entails that you'll ever actually live well. This analogy, though, isn't perfect because, although one may not experience the pain of those diseases even if one doesn't pay the price of disciplining one's physical habits (simply because one is lucky), there's no way to live well without becoming a serious seeker, without living an examined life, without trying to live well. **Mastery never happens accidentally.**

How can we nonsages tell which category someone else is in? It's impossible to know. The only evidence we can have is simply to examine what a person says and does. Sometimes, though, it is seems clear when someone is a master. The Buddha, for example, who spent twenty-nine years in 1, six years in 2 and the last forty-five years of his life in 3, was usually, though not always, recognized during that last period as very, very special by folks he encountered. Also, whenever someone is suffering intensely, it is likely that that person is not a philosopher, because there may be less suffering in 2 and there is little or none in 3.

I admit, though, that there usually is temporarily even more suffering in 2 than in 1; the initial confusion or numbing that occurs when one becomes a philosopher can hurt a lot. Remember the eaglet.[5] So don't be shocked if your initial exposure to philosophy worsens your identity

The Meditative Approach to Philosophy

crisis. Like beginning an exercise program, though it's initially painful, it is normal and just the price to be paid for the important benefits. (If you are having trouble, please don't hesitate to talk to me or to another philosopher or a clinical psychologist about it.)

The important moral point here is that, since a mistake in categorizing someone else is always possible for us, it's impossible to know that we should treat people differently.

Suppose you are a nonphilosopher wondering whether or not becoming a philosopher is worth the cost. Here's the problem with doing nothing: whether you realize it or not, whether you admit it or not, you are (probably unintentionally) causing suffering [anguish, pervasive unsatisfactoriness, dislocation, dukkha] to yourself and to those around you. The chief reason for this is that you are a slave to your egoistic attachments. It is this that is constantly poisoning your life, continually causing the suffering you are experiencing (although, even if you understand this, you may usually prefer to deny or lie to yourself about it). In your more honest moments, don't you occasionally realize how desperate your situation really is? Don't you admit that you have no idea at all what you are doing, that you are just muddling through life being pulled this way and then that way like all other nonphilosophers? Aren't you drifting? Aren't you spinning your wheels? Do you really think that you have all the answers to life's most important questions? Do you really think that, without even trying, without focused, disciplined, persistent practice of an effective kind, you somehow already automatically know who you are and why you are here and what you should be doing?

The solution is to let go of the egoistic attachments that are causing the difficulty. The root of the problem is ignorance. You are dreaming if you believe either that the self/nonself distinction is ultimate or that mere thinking can overcome it. As a consequence of understanding yourself to be separated from everything else, aren't you constantly and vainly trying to attach yourself to whatever you value (desire, crave, want, prefer) and to protect yourself from whatever you don't value? This way of living cannot work. [See "Gaining and Losing" below.]

It's also likely that either you are already often unhappy, perhaps even suicidal, or are suffering from the "someday syndrome," which is thinking that, "If only I had X, I'd finally begin living well." 'X' stands for whatever egoistic satisfactions you crave—a certain person as a lover, an academic degree, a job, financial wealth, health, a family of your own, a house, a career, retirement, travel, the grace of God, whatever.

You think, in other words, that you lack something essential to living well and that it is possible to gain what you lack. That is always false; it's a delusion of the greatest magnitude. It's the chief reason why you are incessantly harming yourself and others. That will never even begin to change until you become a philosopher and free yourself from your predicament. In other words, although you cannot know this for yourself while remaining a nonphilosopher and there may even be cases in which it may not be true, my experience is that life as a philosopher, despite its initial shock, hurts a lot less than life as a nonphilosopher. How could you find out for yourself? There's only one way. All philosophers recommend it!

Please do not misunderstand: my suggestion is hypothetical, not categorical. I do not urge you to become a philosopher. Instead, if you are not a philosopher and you are hurting, if your life isn't working well, if you are suffering too much, then I urge you to make the only change that could work, namely, to become a philosopher seriously seeking liberation.

Becoming a philosopher is a significant achievement. Many folks appear never to attain it, even though, with effective guidance, someone with determination and ability can attain it in a matter of weeks, often in just two or three months. The chief reason being a serious seeker feels better than remaining stuck as a nonphilosopher is that a philosopher realizes that he or she is no longer forced to live poorly; in other words, unlike a nonphilosopher, a philosopher at least has a chance of living well. Living well without even trying to live well is impossible. Either one commits wholeheartedly to philosophy, or one lives poorly. Suicide and living poorly (mediocrity, living a settle-for life) are the only alternatives to committing to excellence.

What does an-as-yet-unsuccessful philosopher do? Practices seeking! In the western tradition, Socrates is the paradigmatic philosopher: he continually challenged himself and those around him to live better. He thought of himself as a gadfly whose mission in live was to sting others into living better. He often annoyed or angered nonphilosophers. As a result, there came a time when those who had political power wanted to get rid of him and he was coerced into committing suicide.

Contrary to myth, philosophers are not popular with nonphilosophers. They are often resented and sometimes killed. If you become a philosopher, you may try to stimulate nonphilosophers to help themselves by adopting examined lives, but many would resent you for doing that. Far from being universally admired, in practice philosophers are often hated by nonphilosophers because philosophers are often (correctly!) thought of as being a dangerous threat to nonphilosophers who prefer to be left alone to waste their lives as slaves to their egoistic attachments. Because of this, unless they are somehow rewarded for doing it, some philosophers don't emulate Socrates by continually challenging others and either withdraw to the companionship of only other philosophers or become hermits.

Seeking, living in 2, is only transitional. 2 is necessary to attain 3. One should spend as little time in 2 as possible. It's easy to get stuck merely thinking, especially if one becomes a master thinker. However, thinking well is not living well, and thinking well is insufficient for living well. It's easy to get too comfortable and to adjust to a settle-for life even in 2. Even though living an examined life does not free one from pervasive unsatisfactoriness, it can significantly decrease it. Instead of increasing one's desire to finish the job by eliminating it, that decrease itself can make life so enjoyable that one gets stuck in 2 and fails to pay the price for pushing on—at least until one gets jolted by some crisis or other. Then it's time to practice much more intensely and persistently.

Anyone egoistically attached to anything is in 1 or 2. Even life in 2 is poisoned by attachment; even a serious seeker wants something else, namely, to live well. Even a serious seeker suffers by craving something not present.

Just as there are different ways of living an examined life in 2, there may be different ways of growing from 2 to 3.

The Meditative Approach to Philosophy

The only effective general one I have discovered, however, is leading a life of meditation, which is the topic of this book. Even serious seekers tend to get distracted by, for example, regrets or fond memories about the past or by hopes and fears about the future. The truth is that, since yesterday is history and tomorrow is a mystery, the present moment is all we have to work with.

Meditation is valuable for increasing "mindfulness"; it does that by strengthening one's ability to concentrate and by focusing that improved concentration on the present moment. By all accounts, according to everyone who does it, living "mindfully" is better than living forgetfully. However, living "mindfully" is still only an experience within 2; in other words, living "mindfully" is not the same as living well. True, living "mindfully" is much better than living forgetfully—some even use the word 'thrilling' to describe it—but there's a final difficult step to be taken.

What is it? It's probably best described by turning "mindfulness" on the idea of the self. At this level of intense examination and insight, what happens is that the idea of the self dissolves and, so, do all egoistic attachments. This is "awakening." This radical nonattachment permits liberation or freedom, equanimity, peace, and abiding joy.

The critical difference between a 2 and a 3 is that only 3's have awakened to reality directly (in other words, nonconceptually). This permits "enlightenment" ("realization"). Conceptualizing it well without experiencing it is impossible. There are degrees of awakening and enlightenment, but even a initial "faint," "shallow," or "partial" awakening is sufficient to indicate the threshold. With continued practice, awakening "deepens" and pervades all activities, which is enlightenment. A fully enlightened sage always lives well.

The important point here is always to avoid thinking that you understand what living well is like without experiencing it. If you really want to understand it for yourself, practice mastery! Genuinely mastering life is as difficult as it is valuable.

If asked to point out someone who lives well (a sage, a 3), a nonphilosopher would probably point to some saint or other. What is saintliness? This much is sufficient: all saints are selfless. They are not deluded by the self/nonself distinction. If so, this would explain why they are so giving, so loving. They are able to love unconditionally, which is the only genuine kind of love, because they lack any temptation to use others for their own selfish purposes. They don't "see" any essential separation between themselves and other beings. If so, they understand deeply that there's nothing to gain, nothing to achieve. How could there be anything to crave? How could they suffer from the poisons of egoistic attachments? Unlike those of us who are still asleep, they awake to and deeply experience the interconnectedness of all beings. This explains their serenity.

It is not necessary to achieve complete dissolution of the self to become a sage; I believe that there have been only a very few people in the history of the world who have attained the summit of saintliness. The goal is to achieve it most of the time.

To provide one concrete example, in Zen training shallow enlightenment experiences are sometimes overvalued; it is as possible to get as attached or stuck to them as to anything else. Ultimately, they are just experiences. What really counts is how one lives, and living well occurs only with the successful transformation that incessant practice brings after an initial awakening experience. Sages (though not necessarily at every moment unless they are fully enlightened) live awakened lives that flow. The reason why life seems to us 1's and 2's a constant struggle and why we frequently get stuck is because we haven't yet paid the price to become sages, to master life.

What really characterizes **sages** is that they **live detached** (nonattached) lives. It is our egoistic attachments that cause our sufferings. As long as we remain in 1 or 2 we think of ourselves as independent continuant substrata separated from everything else in the world, which includes everything we crave; so naturally we waste our lives trying to gain (possess) those "external" objects that will permanently satisfy us. Such lives always fail to yield the lasting, thorough satisfaction we crave; in other words, they don't work well. (This is why, for example, relationships like utility sex affairs don't work.) Eventually, even many folks stuck in 1 figure this out by wearing out their "if onlies". If only I had a candy bar I'd be happy, or if only I could have sex with her (or him or them), or if only I had more money, or if only I had good children, or if only I had a better job, or if only my spouse were a better person, or if only I could retire and fish all the time, and so on. Then what do they do? Many, unfortunately, seem to settle into lives of, using Thoreau's words, "quiet desperation" or, using Freud's words, "common unhappiness"; they live out their settle-for lives and die. Many commit suicide (in various ways including by becoming addicts of different kinds).

Others wrest themselves away from the common herd by becoming philosophers and seriously seek a better way to live. Some spend the rest of their lives seeking (and I may be one of those). Other philosophers become sages. Sages are the only humans who lead blissful lives without suffering, liberated loving lives of detachment, peace, equanimity, and lasting joy. They are the only masters of living well.

Living in 3 is better than living in 1. Since living in 2 is a necessary condition for living in 3, living in 2 is better than living in 1.

Any normal human being can become a sage. Will you? That depends upon what you decide to do with your life. Liberation from duality is an option. That's the good news. If you are willing to discipline (train, purify, still) your mind to wrest control of your life from all the many forces of slavery and attachment, you can liberate yourself. The bad news? Liberation is difficult. Either way, the outcome of your life is up to you.

Most folks never even become philosophers, and sages are few and far between. Whether that's due to ignorance or laziness or fear or something else, I don't know. What difference does it make? The Buddha used this analogy: if you have an arrow sticking in you, if you think too much about explaining how it got there, you'll die; instead, what you should do is to remove the arrow and dress the wound to permit it to heal. An arrow of attachment is sticking in all of us who are living in 1 or 2. What are you doing about your arrow?

It's important to stress that, essentially, no human being is better than any other human being. Our essential nature is the same. 1's never try to realize it. 2's try but fail. 3's succeed. Even if this 1/2/3 categorization were adequate, there's no essential difference among individuals in the three categories. This is because, to put it one way, the concept of an individual dissolves upon serious examination or, to put it another way, because of the impermanence and interconnectedness of all individuals. Individuals are made up of non-individual parts, namely, qualities. A self is nothing but a cluster of qualities, and qualities are commonalities. So it is false that ultimately separate selves exist, which is why each of us is of infinite value. We are one. The ethical lesson? Treat everyone as a sage or potential sage. Treat everyone else as well as you treat yourself.

Suppose you are in 1 and want to waste no more life: what should you do? I don't know. Nobody knows![6] It is for you to work out your own destiny. However, I'll hazard two initial suggestions here.

First, beginning today, work deliberately every day to improve your attitude. Adopt the attitude of a philosopher.[7] Accept the fact that you alone are responsible for your attitude. Decide to believe that you are infinitely valuable and that you bear sole responsibility for the quality of your life. Decide to trust yourself and begin serious questioning. Here's a classic description of the right way to seek by a successful philosopher (namely, the Buddha[8]):

> "Do not be satisfied with hearsay or with traditions or with legendary lore or with what has come down in scriptures or with conjecture or with logical inference or with weighing evidence or with liking for a view after pondering over it or with someone else's ability or with the thought 'The monk is our teacher.' When you know in yourselves: 'These things are wholesome, blameless, commended by the wise, and being adopted and put into effect they lead to welfare and happiness,' then you should practice and abide in them . . ."

Second, begin immediately everyday to free yourself from bondage to your ego-I by working to loosen all your particular egoistic attachments by clinging less. The easiest and quickest way to do this is to diminish seriously your regular associations with those in 1 and to increase them greatly with those in 2 and 3. Why?

Over time, our environments have a great impact on us, so, if you want to begin to live better, stop letting your environment control you by taking control of it. Surround yourself with philosophers, preferably sages. Live with other philosophers, or at least live in solitude and read books by and about successful philosophers. Practice philosophy incessantly. Separating yourself (temporarily) from nonphilosophers, from those who aren't even trying to live well, makes progress much easier. What could be more important than living well? Since, minimally, every normal human being has the option of wholeheartedly trying to live well, there are no acceptable excuses for failing to try. Either you'll condemn yourself to a wasted life, or you'll get all your 'buts' out of the way and do whatever it takes to liberate yourself and show others the way. Though the way to wisdom is difficult, it is possible to live well.

If you are not already a philosopher, why not become one? Why not give yourself a chance to live well? Why not be as kind as possible to yourself? Why not adopt the goal of becoming a sage?

Aren't you worth it? Aren't you infinitely valuable? Why not simply decide that you are and begin to live as if everything you do matters?

The Meditative Approach to Philosophy

―――――――――――――

Sidebar quotation from Roshi Philip Kapleau: "The teachers you remember with gratitude are not those who made it easy for you but the ones who compassionately gave you a hard, painful time."

―――――――――――――

Attitude

Do you want to make the most from the opportunity you have to grow based on this book you have purchased? I want that for you.

If you do also, it's critical, as the Buddha recommends, to adopt a philosopher's attitude.

An attitude is a set of judgments (beliefs). We are solely responsible for our own attitudes. To become excellent, we should deliberately reject beliefs that inhibit thought and accept beliefs that foster it.

Ultimately, the quality of your thinking will determine the degree of excellence you enjoy in your life. Why?

The results you obtain are the products of your behaviors, and your behaviors are the products of your thinking. This explains why there is no living well without good thinking. Living poorly is an excellent reason, and perhaps the only excellent reason, for beginning to study philosophy. Nobody ever lives well, or even just thinks well, accidentally; always, mastery requires intense, sustained practice of the right kind. (Can you think of even a single exception?) Attitude greatly affects practice. Challenge yourself regularly to improve your attitude. The best time to do it is daily during your morning routine.

Sidebar quotation from Galileo: "You cannot teach a man anything; you can only help him to find it within himself."

Negatively, for example, avoid believing that indirect criticism from these writings means disrespect. **Intellectual progress occurs *only* when ideas clash.** If I am to encourage you to grow as a thinker, I must challenge your ideas in order to encourage you to examine them more closely. You have, in effect, paid me to encourage you to do better, and my efforts would be worthless unless I am able to identify how you could do better. Without weakening your attachments to old ideas, examining them, and, when appropriate, letting them go, you'll never grow.

Positively, for example, give up being afraid to think for yourself. Be willing to **question everything**—including your own ideas, your friends' ideas, your parents' ideas, my ideas, and even the ideas of such intellectual and spiritual giants as Plato and the Buddha.

Admit to yourself that thinking well is difficult and approach it with humility and an open mind. Treat your intellectual intuitions tenderly and learn how to foster them in the ways that work best for you. Try to develop intellectual breadth and coherence as well as depth. Be willing to pay the price for success, which usually involves an increase in solitude and greater estrangement

The Meditative Approach to Philosophy

from nonseekers. Be patient when thinking hard about fundamental ideas. Also, at least if they request it, always be ready to encourage others to think better for themselves.

You've **nothing to lose** in using the ideas from these writings to challenge your own ideas. If your ideas withstand the challenge, good—you can have more confidence in your judgments. If you ideas don't withstand the challenge, good—you can replace your judgments with better ones.

Deliberately acting as a master thinker can, with regular practice, help you to become a master thinker—just as, for example, deliberately forcing yourself to act as a master (complete) friend, even if you don't happen to feel like it, can, with regular practice, help you to become a master friend. Don't wait for enthusiasm to strike in order to begin productive activity; instead, just start engaging in productive activity and enthusiasm will come.

Can becoming a philosopher really enable you to live better? The opportunity for finding out for yourself is right in front of you. Why not commit yourself wholeheartedly to finding out? How could anything else be more important? Make the critically important judgment that your life is worth living and then determine for yourself if improved thinking can help you to live better.

Action dissolves fear. It's O.K. to make a mistake; mistakes are how we learn. **Just make small mistakes, and don't repeat a mistake.**. Take action—even just a small step—daily in the direction you want to go.

In my judgment, the Buddha was the greatest philosopher who ever lived. Meditation is critical to understanding the Buddha's chief ideas; someone who does not meditate is someone who cannot understand them.

———————

Sidebar quotation from The Buddha: "There is no meditation for one lacking insight, no insight in one who does not meditate."

———————

Remember, the Buddha, like all philosophers, is interested in living well—not just in thinking well. Like the Buddha, I believe that it is impossible to live well without mastering some effective spiritual practice or other (such as zazen).

———————

Sidebar quotation from Roshi Shunryu Suzuki: "Unless you know how to practice zazen, no one can help you."

———————

Why not be as kind to yourself as possible and give yourself the great gift of daily meditation?

16

Serious Personal Problems

It's possible that you happen to have serious problems to deal with before actually following the Buddha's advice.

DEPRESSION

Have you recently been in a depressed mood most of the time nearly every day? Have you recently had diminished interest or enjoyment in activities most of the time nearly every day? Has your body weight recently dropped due to poor appetite or has it gone up due to increased appetite? Are you having difficulty sleeping or sleeping too much? Have you lost energy? Are you fatigued? Do you feel worthless, excessively guilty, or hopeless? Has your ability to concentrate diminished? Do you recurrently think about death or suicide?

If your answers to some of these questions are affirmative, you may be suffering from major depression or even undiagnosed major depression, which is a common disorder in our society. Since, fortunately, it's usually an eminently treatable disorder that often has serious consequences, please be kind to yourself and seek clinical treatment. (Incidentally, in the long term, nothing—I believe—will be more valuable for you than the Buddha's prescription.)

Also, the booklist at the end of The 7 Steps to Mastery has some very helpful readings about curing mood disorders. It may surprise you to learn that some have physical causes that can be treated by something as simple as targeted, temporary supplementation and a permanently improved diet.

SUICIDE

Suicide is the eighth leading cause of death in our population. In people aged 15 to 24, it's the third leading cause of death.

You are at increased risk if you have suffered family trauma, unstabilized turmoil, domestic violence, physical or sexual abuse, loss of a family member, feelings of being a burden, or had an alcoholic parent. Are you depressed? Do you feel hopeless? Furthermore, associated contributing factors may be indicated by affirmative answers to any of the following questions: Are you isolated or withdrawn? Do you use alcohol, marijuana, or cocaine? If you are a student, is your academic performance poor? Do you frequently get into disputes with your peers? Have you been disappointed romantically? Are you worried about pregnancy, sexual orientation, or AIDS? Are you upset about the suicide of any friends, peers, or family members? Do you suffer from cancer, Huntington's disease, MS, or anorexia nervosa? Have you had a head or spinal cord injury? Have you ever attempted suicide?

Suicidal crises are episodic. Definitive treatment does cause them to pass. If you find yourself thinking about suicide, please be kind to yourself and seek expert help. Treat such obstacles as opportunities to teach yourself how to live better. You are capable of living well, so why not teach yourself how? If you do, you'll not only benefit yourself, but also you'll be able to show others how to help themselves.

Paying the Price

Always, one must pay the price.

Everything we do has a price: if we do one thing, we can't be doing another. If you teach yourself how to take good care of the present moment by using a spiritual practice (such as the one taught below), you can chart a successful future. How is that possible? It's because what you do in the present moment today determines how well you may live tomorrow, just as what you have done in the past is determining how well you are living today.

Living well doesn't happen by luck or magic or chance. If you are to begin living well, you must pay the price for doing so. The initial key is to take responsibility for the quality of your own life. The choices that you make every day concerning your thoughts, speech, and actions determine the quality of your life. In particular, your attitude is solely your responsibility. If you have been living poorly, why not use that itself as motivation to live better, to become a philosopher?

Doing so involves the unpopular alternative of thinking seriously about your values, which determine your choices. If you don't, you'll continue to suffer; if you do, you can begin to break the grip of pervasive dissatisfaction (anguish, dislocation, suffering, <u>dukkha</u>) permanently.

Even if you accept full responsibility for your own life (instead of blaming your parents or friends or teachers or society or genes or whatever), decide what you want, and wholeheartedly commit yourself to doing whatever it takes, you'll need to change. Unless you improve what you've been doing, you'll continue to get similar results.

Sidebar quotation from John Fuhrman: "If you are unwilling to change, you have already reached your maximum potential."

One cannot do better without growing. The trouble with growing is that it's always uncomfortable and usually painful, which explains why many people do as little of it as possible. To avoid leaving their comfort zones, many cling to their habitual thoughts, speech, and activities.

The price of not growing, the price of remaining a slave to egoistic attachments, is the elimination of the possibility of living well. Why? We live in the domain of becoming[9]; we do not inhabit the static domain of being. **Nothing abides.** Impermanence is reality. Hence, clinging to what-is never works because what-is is always in transition (ceaseless flux).

The Meditative Approach to Philosophy

Therefore, if you are serious about living well, you'll avoid a no-growth policy at all costs. In fact, you'll **deliberately and habitually challenge yourself to grow**. Instead of fearing change, you'll embrace it! In this context, what could be more important than deciding what you really value and actively going for it?

Though I hope that you do, it is not necessary for you to like me personally or anything about me (such as my writing style) to benefit greatly from this book. Why?

I'm not the subject matter: the ideas presented here are all about *your* living better. You are the focus. I am merely a messenger; it's the message that's important.

Our personalities are probably of different types.[10] That doesn't matter. You are what matters.

Please be kind to yourself. That's the opposite of being hard on yourself, which is what you may be doing without realizing it. That's precisely what you are doing if you are trying to live well without meditating daily

Apprehending[11]

To apprehend conceptually is to employ our epistemic capacities in an effort to understand reality. Reality (what-is) is truth. There is no guarantee that it is possible to conceptualize reality correctly, but it is obviously important to come as close as possible.

Ordinary thought and speech seem to regard believing and knowing as the two modes of apprehending; if so, this requires revision.

With respect to beliefs, where 'p' stands for some proposition, it is senseless to make statements such as "I am believing that p." Beliefs are not occurrences. (Since there are no occurrent beliefs, a belief cannot be a disposition to assent to an occurrent belief.) Epistemologists have had great difficulty answering the question, 'What is a belief?' (If that surprises you, just try answering it clearly for yourself!) Without a clear answer to this question, let's set aside the notion of believing.

Instead, let's focus on judgments. We regularly experience being conscious of a (real or unreal) state of affairs (proposition, fact, situation), and that is all that an occurrent judgment is. A judgment is a direct mental relation to a (real or unreal) state of affairs; judgments are either occurrent or dispositions to engage in such episodes of consciousness. Judgments are familiar, distinctive, unquestionable, and not further analyzable.

Making judgments is independent of evidence (justification). A simplistic, straightforward voluntarism in this context is false. For example, if I'm walking across a road and suddenly notice that a truck is rapidly approaching, I am hardly at liberty to choose to refrain from that judgment or not.

On the other hand, if I claim to know that p, then evidence is required. What is evidence required for knowledge?

Demonstrative evidence is incompatible with the falsehood of the judgment it is evidence for. What is demonstrative evidence?

If Butchvarov is correct, the phenomenological rock bottom here is the brute psychological fact of one's finding it unthinkable that one is mistaken in judging the particular proposition in question to be true. Knowledge is the unthinkability of mistake or error.[12]

The relevant unthinkability is neither vague nor abstract, and it is neither purely conceptual nor purely logical; instead, it is the inability by a particular person at a particular time and in a particular context to think there is a mistake about a particular proposition.

If so, the unthinkability of mistake does not entail truth; the unthinkability of mistake is not the same as infallibility, which trivially entails truth. However, since what is unthinkable is one's not apprehending truth, the unthinkability of mistake is the closest we can come epistemically and conceptually to truth.

The unthinkability of mistake is self-validating. Why? Appealing to the phenomenological rock bottom experience guarantees genuine self-evidence; the brute psychological fact is epistemically critical. How could there be any circularity or infinite regress?

Nondemonstrative evidence, on the other hand, is compatible with the falsehood of the judgment it is the evidence for. The concept of nondemonstrative evidence is useless, inapplicable. Why? It lacks a phenomenological ground. It's a conceptual phantom. There is, at least so far, no concept of epistemic probability.

If so, this undermines any supposedly articulate understanding of rationality or rational belief or probable belief. This consequence is very important in ethics and political philosophy as well as in the philosophy of science. This grounds the important claim, which is made multiple times in The 7 Steps to Mastery, that **there is no knowledge about right and wrong** as well as the even more important claim that **there is no rational belief about right and wrong!**

Our ability to apprehend reality conceptually is restricted (and perhaps distorted), which is a point that many monists and mystics have made.

Might nonconceptual apprehension be unrestricted (and perhaps undistorted)? This, truly, is an exciting possibility.

The Two Methods of Philosophy

If the argument in the previous section is correct, we lack both knowledge and rational belief about what is right or wrong to do.

There is no more important problem!

Our ability to apprehend reality (in other words, to know or have rational belief about what-is) is severely restricted and, perhaps, distorted. The distortion comes from our concepts, but we are unable to conceptualize without concepts.

This is not original: many monists and mystics have made this point.

Let's think more about it.

A philosopher is someone who is seriously trying to live well (to become a 3, to be wise, to be a sage). Philosophers have existed in various cultures around the world for at least 2500 years.

Living well is being and doing well, and that requires valuing well. Values do not exist apart from everything else; what-is (reality) includes values.

The philosophic tradition encompasses two distinct approaches to apprehending what-is. There is no standard terminology for describing them. The following remarks are merely signposts (pointings).

UNDERSTANDING

The method of (conceptual) <u>understanding</u> is dominant in the western philosophic tradition. Socrates is the paradigmatic western philosopher. To understand what-is is to conceptualize it correctly.

As explained in <u>The 7 Steps to Mastery</u>[13], a concept is a principle of classification. Understanding is conceptual [discursive, classificatory, discriminatory] thinking. To conceptualize well it is necessary to engage in dialectic, the give and take of argument that is inseparable from thinking hard about analogies, from noticing relevant similarities and differences. Developing understanding requires persistence as well as rigorous intellectual effort; it is always a gradual process.

It always proceeds on the basis of the logic of noncontradiction [where 'F' is some concept, an object cannot both be F and not be F] and the identity principle that an object is what it is and is not another object.

The Meditative Approach to Philosophy

The chief philosophic difficulty with respect to the method of understanding is that it seems impotent to yield wisdom. Even though there can be knowledge of [abstract] good and evil, there cannot be knowledge of [concrete] right and wrong (because the consequences of an action are relevant to its moral evaluation and it is always impossible to know all the consequences of an action). Worse, without a solution to the problem of rational belief (see the previous section), this method cannot provide any guidance whatsoever about what to do. In short, understanding well cannot yield living well.

The chief intellectual difficulty with respect to the method of understanding is that understanding may be falsification. This is an argument raised by some western monists. What-is seems to be neither F nor not-F but both F and not-F. In other words, concepts inevitably distort reality.

INSIGHT

The method of insight (direct experience) is dominant in the eastern philosophic tradition. The Buddha is the paradigmatic eastern philosopher. Insight is the nonconceptual apprehension of what-is. In principle, although an initial insight or awakening can be deepened with the right kind of practice (such as meditation) into enlightenment, an initial insight cannot be developed: it is sudden. The right kind of practice (such as meditation) may make initial insight more likely, but the enlightenment experience itself is not a cumulative one; rather it is a mental cataclysm.

What-is is nonconceptualized reality. Since language is used solely in order to reveal the "emptiness" that transcends conceptualization and contradictions may be useful for doing that, the method of insight permits contradictions as well as the identity principle that an object which is not itself is truly itself. Only the enlightened are able to live well. Although many are not awake, we are all inherently enlightened.

The chief philosophic difficulty with respect to the method of insight is that it isn't clear what to do to obtain it. Is sitting in meditation the means to obtaining enlightenment (which seems foolish since wouldn't the future enlightenment experience always be beyond the present sitting experience?) or is it already enlightenment (which would automatically make anyone who "sits", however briefly or poorly, enlightened!)?

Also, doesn't engaging in the practice of meditation require an argument? How could we know or have rational belief that we ought to meditate? After all, we lack both knowledge and rational belief that we ought to engage in any particular kind of action.

The chief intellectual difficulty with respect to the method of insight is obvious: enlightenment is unintelligible. Since it is indescribable, how could one even recognize an enlightenment experience as genuine? Also, how could one be enlightened and not realize it?

DISCUSSION

The Meditative Approach to Philosophy

Some serious philosophers are partisans of the method of understanding and reject the method of insight completely, whereas some serious philosophers are partisans of the method of insight and reject the method of understanding completely.

Even if the two methods are not mutually exclusive, since life is short, there is an initial difficulty: time spent engaging in the dialectic, in conceptual thinking, is not time spent engaging in meditation, in nonconceptual awareness.

Lurking here is an important issue. Please ask yourself this serious, important question: **"How should I live my life?"**

I happen to believe that it's best to investigate this for ourselves. Philosophers who are not yet sages (in other words, 2's) would be wise to expose themselves thoroughly to both methods. Why? Though the situation may appear hopeless, it may not actually be hopeless. It may be that we simply haven't proceeded far enough to apprehend what we need to apprehend to live well.

Exposure to a method means practicing it—not just thinking about it. In particular, it is not enough merely to think about meditation. Why? Well, could you really understand an orgasm without ever having experienced one? Could you appreciate what a pineapple tastes like without ever having ever tasted one? An experience is not the same as a description of an experience.

It is at least possible that the methods are complementary. Though both methods cannot be practiced simultaneously (although one can be fully absorbed for periods of time in the dialectic), it is possible that the same person could be both a master of the dialectic and a meditation master.

By way of analogy, why couldn't, for example, the same person be both a master swimmer and a master poet? Why couldn't someone be both a master bodybuilder and a master physicist? Furthermore, it's at least possible that the physical training involved in becoming or being an excellent swimmer or bodybuilder might enhance one's ability to excel intellectually or artistically.

There is nothing more important than living well. (Notice that, if you disagreed, you'd have to specify what is more important than living well—and that would merely be your conception of living well.) This issue about how to do it is critical.

Philosophers have never recommended some third method for living well in addition to the method of understanding and the method of insight. It seems to me very likely that, in over 2500 years, philosophers would have noticed such a third method if there were one. I, at least, am not aware of one.

Someone who is inexperienced in making money is not someone you should rely on for guidance about making money. Someone who is inexperienced in reading poetry is not someone you should rely on for guidance about appreciating poetry. Someone who is inexperienced as an auto mechanic is not someone you should rely on for guidance about repairing your defective automobile. Someone who is not licensed as a physician is not someone you should rely on for guidance about diagnosing which illness you have. In each case, you'd be wiser to rely on a master. Ultimately, though, what you do is your decision.

That's the most important problem with life: we constantly have to make decisions about what to do and be without knowing or having rational belief about how to make them well!

Someone who has not demonstrated a mastery of the dialectic is not someone I would rely on for advice about the dialectic, and someone who has not demonstrated a mastery of meditation is not someone I would rely on for advice about meditation. (If I myself am not an expert, recognizing an expert is always a problem.) If I want assistance on evaluating each, I should try to find someone who has mastered both.

Should you pay any attention whatsoever to the ideas I'm promoting? Not necessarily.

My attempt here as well as in <u>The Three Things the Rest of Us Should Know about ZEN TRAINING</u> and in <u>The 7 Steps to Mastery</u> is to encourage you to find out for yourself. My understanding and insight are limited. My role is to stimulate you into finding out for yourself. Please do the thinking and do the meditating! There's no other way.

The Ideal Philosopher

The ideal philosopher is one who masters both the method of understanding and the method of insight. The perfect philosopher would be one who is a master thinker as well as a master meditator.

It's important not to confuse the ideal with the real. Still, having heroes is valuable. It's good to have models to emulate. It's one of the traditional ways we encourage and challenge ourselves to live better.

Why not adopt such a hero? One's never too old for heroes.

My hero is The Buddha. It's not just that he was a spiritual genius; everyone understands that. He was also a master thinker. That is the inescapable conclusion of anyone who has taken the trouble to read some of the major sutras.

(It's true that he didn't himself write any books. A sufficient reason for that is that he didn't want people fanatically attaching to his ideas; instead, he was always concerned to have us find out for ourselves. Nevertheless, many of his teachings were preserved orally for generations and eventually written down. It is impossible to read many of these teachings with understanding and not conclude that The Buddha was a master dialectician.)

As far as I've been able to determine, The Buddha was the most successful philosopher who ever lived. I'm not claiming that he was perfect. He, too, suffered from our shared human condition.

Furthermore, I'm not suggesting that he should be your hero. All I'm suggesting is that you pick someone to emulate who was both a master thinker and a master meditator.

You might even personally know someone who is both. If so, you are very lucky indeed. If not, no matter: do some investigation and select someone appropriate. Doing so can really help.

Gaining and Losing

We all want to be happy. The important question is, "How?"

Sometimes folks think that there are different ways to happiness, that my way of being happy might be different from your way of being happy. This is not true. As Aristotle emphasizes, we are all of the same kind: we are all human beings. How could it be that what is good for one human being is different from what is good for another human being? What is good for, say, a tree or a star may differ from what is good for a human being, but, since we humans are all of the same sort, what is good for me is the same as what is good for you. What is good for us is happiness.

Though there are many ways of living. However, there are only two ultimate ways (paths, processes, directions): the way of gaining and the way of losing.

THE WAY OF GAINING

This is also called the way of attachment or accumulation or achievement or desiring. It is the nonspiritual path to living well.

Most people seek happiness by trying to accumulate goods.

(i) They may try to accumulate goods by various processes of self-development designed to achieve "internal" goods (such as more conceptual understanding or virtue or fitness).

(ii) They may try to accumulate goods from "external" sources such as other people (such as friendships or love affairs or families or esteem), material goods (such as money or possessions [like real estate or art]), or experiences (such as traveling or attaching to the idea of God).

(iii) They may seek both internal and external goods.

This path is based on the judgment that I will become happy if only I am able to attach myself to (accumulate, achieve, gain) things that will benefit me. The more and better goods I accumulate, the happier I shall be.

This path presupposes that I am separate from what is good for me. Since this is false, this method doesn't work. It can't work!

Not only doesn't this path work, it perpetuates suffering. "What will a man gain by winning the whole world, at the cost of his true self?"[14] Nothing! There is nothing to gain!

The implicit distinction here is the distinction between one's false self and one's true self: one's false self is thought to be separate from everything else, whereas one's true self is everything!

The Meditative Approach to Philosophy

Since suffering is caused by separation, as long as one clings tightly to one's idea of oneself as separate, one is perpetuating a (delusional) split between oneself and everything else. How could such a split be overcome by somehow attaching oneself to goods that are separate from oneself? The truth is that there is no (separate) self to do any attaching; furthermore, the goods one desires (such as another lover or a better child or more money) are themselves transitory.

The way of attachment is the way of desiring (wanting, craving), which is a dead end. Why? Ask yourself: what is the good with respect to any desire? It is the annihilation of the desire, which is nothing. For example, the good with respect to hunger, which is the desire for food, is not food but the elimination of the hunger. This explains why the way of gaining satisfactions doesn't work. Desire only breeds more desire.

The way of attachment is the way that children live. They think "If only I had X, I'd be happy", and then they try to gain X. Even if successful in gaining X, the satisfaction, like X itself, is temporary; almost immediately they want Y and then Z and so on. Immature adults simply continue this process of life as an endless quest to get whatever it is they want—and then they die without ever being happy.

Egocentric attachments are poisons. One who is a slave to them is like one who is content to dream one's way through life, like one who prefers fantasy to reality; such a one usually misses the present moment, which is the only moment when life may be lived. By way of contrast, mature adults learn from experience that the way of attachment doesn't work. If they are philosophers, instead of settling for lives of incessant distractions and suffering, they search for a better way.

THE WAY OF LOSING

This is also called the way of nonattachment or letting go or renunciation or surrendering. It is the spiritual path to living well.

A few people seek happiness by detachment. They deliberately stop practicing the way of desiring; they begin practicing letting go of the idea that happiness is the result of accumulating goods.

When successful, unlike children, they no longer suffer from the someday syndrome ("if only I had X, I'd be happy"). In fact, those who are wholly successful no longer desire anything! They don't want to be or do or have anything—including happiness! In other words, they are not attached to anything. They are desireless. (Please avoid evaluating this without experiencing its peacefulness.)

This path presupposes that it is false that I am separate from what is good for me. I am not something separate from reality: I am reality! In other words, the world is my true self, which is what mystics have always said. There's no separate self to do any attaching—and nothing separate to be attached to! Everything necessary for me to live well is available right here, right now. The only requirement for happiness is that I realize it.

The Meditative Approach to Philosophy

By way of contrast, the only other option cannot work. Attaching to the idea of my false self assumes a fundamental bifurcation between me and everything else. Such separation is the most important delusion. Why? Suffering is optional! Letting go of the separation is letting go of suffering (such as greed, fear, anger, and loneliness). Instead of perpetuating suffering, successful implementation of the way of nonattachment wholly eliminates suffering. The more letting go I do, the less suffering I experience and, so, the happier I am. Less greed means more happiness!

This requires practice. Why? Since we falsely believe that, if we let go we'll lose the goods that make us happy, we are afraid to let go. The reality, though, is that, the more we let go, the happier we become. See for yourself! Wouldn't it be foolish to evaluate it without experiencing it?

The way of nonattachment is the way that sages (mature adults, successful philosophers) live. They live like those who have awakened from a dream. They live well.

Transition

Anyone who remains attached to the way of gaining will remain perpetually dissatisfied. Such a person is always imagining the greater happiness involved if only gaining X were to occur. In other words, such a person is always dissatisfied in the present moment.

If you are serious about living well, it's because you are dissatisfied with the way of gaining. Your task is to transition from the way of gaining to the way of losing. If you succeed in making the transition, your dissatisfaction will have had the greatest possible beneficial consequence.

This is where the method of insight becomes critical. There is simply no way to think yourself from the method of gaining to the method of losing. Even a master dialectician is helpless with respect to this transition.

Just as it is impossible to master a sport or a musical instrument merely by thinking about it, so it is impossible to master the transition from the way of gaining to the way of losing merely by thinking about it.

Mastering the way of nonattachment requires mastery of an effective spiritual practice, which explains why it is the spiritual path (as opposed to the nonspiritual path of attachment). It is necessary to discipline (train, purify, still) the mind to be successful. Waking up spiritually requires a spiritual effort.

This is wonderful news!

What if there were no method for successfully making the transition? That would be terrible.

Furthermore, it would also be terrible if spiritual success were simply the result of luck or factors beyond one's control. Instead, if you will do what it takes to realize your true nature, happiness is a genuine possibility. Dissatisfaction is optional!

Furthermore, there are many different kinds of spiritual practices that are effective. It's not as if you must, for example, master zazen or die unrealized. If one practice doesn't work for you, find another that will.

Dissatisfaction

Recall or imagine a time without peace of mind.

Perhaps you failed a test at school, performed badly at a concert, got fired from a job, lost your house, suffered a divorce, experienced the death of a loved one, were diagnosed with a serious illness, or something similar.

How did that make you feel? How well were you able to sleep? Did you rapidly lose or gain weight? Were you unable to concentrate? Did troubling emotions regularly upset your life? We've all been that dissatisfied.

Even now, in fact, there may be nothing more important to you than settling down and attaining more peace of mind. It could be that you are suffering intensely, that you are acutely dissatisfied with your life.

Even if you are only mildly or occasionally dissatisfied, practicing meditation would help.

Dissatisfaction is normal. It's the chief reason why people begin meditating. Unless we wanted an improvement, we wouldn't try anything different. Changing takes effort, and it's natural be to lazy.

If you are interested in learning how to meditate, it's because you are hoping that it will be a way for you to live better. Good! Do it. It will help.

Even if all you want to do is to fall asleep more quickly at night and to sleep more soundly, meditating effectively will help.

How much might it help? It depends upon how well you master whatever meditation technique you select. In my judgment, it's not possible to live well without mastering meditation.

There are two kinds of meditation: "direct" (stilling) and "indirect" (moving).

Examples of direct meditation techniques are: zazen (either following the breath [shikan-taza] or koan training), insight [vipassana] meditation, and rajah yoga.

The Meditative Approach to Philosophy

Examples of indirect meditation techniques are: bhakti yoga, jnana yoga, Quaker quietism, The Kabbalah, and ecstatic prayer.

There are many more examples of each kind.

It's impossible to tell in advance which kind would work best for you. It's also impossible to tell in advance which technique within a kind would work best for you. To find out, you may need to try more than one.

Permit me three cautionary notes before you begin experimenting:

    1. If you are suffering acutely, you may greatly benefit from some professional guidance to work more on yourself before any kind of meditation will benefit you. Your acute dissatisfaction may even prevent you from trying any kind of meditation. If that's your situation, don't despair! You will be able to benefit from meditation, but you've some preliminary work to do first.

    2. When you try a specific meditation technique, give it an honest trial before rejecting it. It's not likely that any technique will work quickly. Guard against impatience.

    3. Avoid sampling two or more meditation techniques simultaneously or combining them into your own unique blend. Unless you happen to be a spiritual genius, such an approach will fail. Humility works. Let a teacher help you.

If you already have a spiritual tradition from which you are not alienated, you may already have access to some meditation technique that might work well from you. [See the next section.]

You may relate to my own story, which my meditation teacher told me is not uncommon. I had read a little about meditation as an undergraduate; it was interesting, but I didn't actually try it. Years later after my partner in a long-term relationship dumped me, I found myself emotionally distraught. I needed some relief, yet I was a spiritual zero. I read about different meditation techniques, and, this time, I took action. I took a course at a local community college on a version of tai chi. I enjoyed the course and was soon able to feel the chi move; however, I didn't have the sense that it was the right path for me. I read The Three Pillars of Zen and began sitting on my own. As soon as I did, I felt that I was home. A few months later, I attended a one-day workshop on zazen and soon thereafter joined a local sangha.

The Meditative Approach to Philosophy

When you, too, have the feeling that you have found a meditation technique that enables you to feel that you are on your way home, you'll know that you've settled on one that will work for you.

If you are hurting and ready to experiment, please do. Be assured: there is a kind of meditation that will work well for you. Your task is simply to locate and master it.

Meditation and Religion

A meditative practice is a spiritual or breathing practice. It is neither religious nor anti-religious; it's nonreligious. The only faith required to begin meditating is that the practice might be beneficial.

Some religious practices are similar to some meditative practices.

Those with monotheistic religious backgrounds naturally wonder about prayer: is prayer an effective meditation technique? If it's the right kind of prayer, it can be.

Unless they are prayers of gratitude or thanksgiving, most prayers seem to be petitions. "Dear God: bring me salvation or cure Tammy of her cancer or feed the hungry or stop the war or help me lose twenty pounds." Petitionary prayer is a request for something the practitioner wants.

Some thinkers have made two critiques about petitionary prayer.

First, it is blasphemous. The practioner is, in effect, displaying the hubris to be trying to tell the Divine what to do!

Second, it is egocentric. It's about some outcome that the practitioner desires. Shouldn't the practitioner be thinking solely about what the Divine desires? In other words, petitionary prayer only serves to reinforce the separation between the practitioner and the Divine.

All egocentric desires are poisons!

One way to understand this is that all dissatisfactions are caused by separation. Unless there is something such as health or food or wealth or love or peace or weight loss that you want and lack, you will not be dissatisfied. **All egocentric desires require dissatisfaction that is based on separation.**

Since petitionary prayer presupposes separation from the Divine, practicing it only reinforces that separation. Therefore, it is counterproductive in terms of curing what ails us. If 'Hell' denotes separation from the Divine, petitionary prayer is a symptom of living in Hell.

On the other hand, prayer that diminishes the distance between the practitioner and the Divine may diminish dissatisfaction. It's called "absolute" prayer, which is prayer the way that mystics pray. Its sole object is overcoming separation by achieving union with the Divine. To live in Heaven is to be one with the Divine.

———

Sidebar quotation from Master Eckhart: "God's being is my life . . . God's is-ness is my is-ness, and neither more nor less."

———

If so, then absolute prayer may be one religious practice that is an effective spiritual practice, which is one that unifies (heals, produces atonement [at-one-ment]).

To succeed, the mystic lets go of self and unites with the Divine.

Perhaps this is what Jesus meant when he said, "If anyone wishes to be a follower of mine, he must leave self behind; day after day he must take up his cross, and come with me."[15] His reference to taking up his cross day after day may be his way of referring to practicing prayer properly day after day. (As Kierkegaard was fond of emphasizing, a few minutes on Sunday mornings won't cut it.)

If absolute prayer, which is prayer as mystics practice prayer, is an effective spiritual practice, note that there's a sense in which it's not a religious practice at all. Mystics are concerned with overcoming separation, and that has nothing essential to do with accepting any kind of religious or supernatural creed. The mystic's achievement is separate from the mystic's religious beliefs. In fact, mystics don't even need any religious beliefs!

So there's a question about whether or not absolute prayer is really a religious practice. Of course, someone who accepts religious beliefs will interpret a mystical experience as union with God, but such an interpretation is distinct from the experience itself.

Letting Go of Self

Is daily practice of some meditative technique required for living well? I think so.

Any standard meditative practice can work for living well. How is this possible?

It's possible because, in order to be mastered, they all are based on the same fundamental idea, namely, that **it is we who are causing our own dissatisfaction**. Living well requires living without dissatisfaction, and living without dissatisfaction requires that we stop creating dissatisfaction.

The only way to stop creating it is to let go of one's attachment to one's self concept. If you want to live well, let go of your egocentricity. It's that simple.

Meditation works because it dissolves egocentricity. By dissolving egocentricity, it fosters unity. Meditation undermines the separation between me and everything else.

To lose attachment to self is to gain everything. **To lose self-absorption is to gain the world.** Letting go of self is gaining everything else.

Losing is the opposite of gaining. Since losing self is gaining everything else, it's better to lose than to gain!

We normally want to gain because we think that gaining will make our lives better. Once we have discovered for ourselves the bitter truth that a life of gaining doesn't work well, what should we do? Do the opposite, which is a life of losing.

Meditation has nothing whatsoever to do with self-improvement; it has everything to do with self-dissolution. Self-improvement is only about improving one's gain/loss ratio. Self-dissolution is about dissolving attachment to our self-concepts. In fact, there is no separate self to improve!

Notice that, without peace of mind, all the gains you can imagine won't make you happy.

There is nothing worth gaining. In truth, there's nothing to gain.

The Meditative Approach to Philosophy

All master meditators tell us that losing all our egocentric attachments is the way to live well. Why not find out for yourself?

It's true that you won't even begin until you have soured on a life of gaining. That, though, is only a matter of time. When you are ripe, don't despair: being practicing meditation!

I explain one way to do that in what follows.

Is it worth it? Stop thinking of what you'll gain from meditation and begin thinking of what you'll lose.

Sidebar quotation from The Buddha: "Someone once asked the Buddha skeptically, 'What have you gained through meditation?' The Buddha replied, 'Nothing at all.' 'Then, Blessed One, what good is it?' 'Let me tell you what I lost through meditation: sickness, anger, depression, insecurity, the burden of old age, the fear of death. That is the good of meditation . . . '"

Beginning Without a Teacher

The best way to master meditation is to apprentice yourself to a meditation master and persistently practice doing exactly whatever that master recommends.

In the beginning, however, you don't know what kind of meditation would work for you. So, even if there happened to be a local master who was willing to take you on, you have no way of knowing that.

Remember that philosophers have two methods (namely, understanding and insight). Though it's insight that interests you with respect to meditation, don't neglect understanding. Keep reading. The more relevant reading you do, the shorter will be the time it takes you to find a suitable master or training facility.

If you are a typical westerner, you have a much better idea how to do the thinking than how to do the meditating. It's quite likely that you are already familiar with the actions (such as reading books and taking courses) that are designed to improve a student's ability to think. Use the understanding gained from that process to get you started meditating.

In fact, that's what you should be doing as you read this book.

Realize that I, too, am a typical westerner in that sense. I've been using the method of understanding in philosophy for about forty-five years, but I've only been using the method of insight since 1994.

I am not a meditation master. I do not know what you should do to master meditation.

What I'm able to do for you, however, is to explain how I understand meditation and report what I've learned about one kind of meditation. That is sufficient to get you started. Once you are regularly reading about meditation and practicing meditation daily, you'll have some experience of your own to use to help you determine how to proceed.

The initial difficulty is critical. It's the initial hump that you must get over to begin practicing daily. If you never get over it, you'll never master meditation. It is my intention that the ideas in this book provide you with everything necessary for you to overcome inertia and begin well.

So what follows is to help you focus on one kind of practice and to provide you with sufficient details so you may, if you choose, start well even on your own.

Spiritual Practice

I knew that I was missing something important, but I didn't know what it was. With the hope that it might help, I began to read about meditation. Having sampled a moving meditation, I wanted to try a stilling meditation.

I settled on the distinctive stilling meditation of Zen, which is called 'zazen.'

It seemed the purest kind of meditation for two reasons. First, unlike moving meditations such as martial arts, it didn't involve learning any new behavioral skills. **Learning how to do zazen is simple.** Physically, it can be learned quite quickly. Second, **the only prerequisite is believing that it might be beneficial..** It doesn't require accepting any religious or supernatural beliefs.

Stilling meditations such as zazen work by a process of concentration (focusing attention fully in the present moment), tranquility (stilling consciousness by letting distracting thoughts go), and insight (awakening). In the west as well as in the east, the way to wisdom has always been through self-examination. Meditation is serious self-examination. I do not believe that living well is possible without it; if so, **if you do not help yourself by mastering an effective spiritual practice, you'll never live well.**

Living well is impossible without liberation, which is the freedom from the pervasive unsatisfactoriness (off-centeredness, anguish, suffering, anxiety, <u>dukkha</u>) that comes from our egocentric attachments. The phrase 'undisciplined freedom' is self-contradictory; there is no genuine liberation without discipline. Mastery of anything requires the discipline that ultimately results in optimal or flow experiences.

Egocentric attachments require the self/other distinction. Letting go of ego dissolves that distinction. That is the selflessness that results from mastering a spiritual practice such as zazen. It's the beginning of living well. Letting go is a simple but difficult process.

However, what could be more worth doing? Try thinking of it this way: the only alternative is infinitely worse. Why settle for a life of nearly incessant dissatisfaction?

A spiritual practice is both a means and an end. Done properly, it is wholly absorbing. It is not anti-intellectual but nonintellectual; it simply does not involve conceptual (discriminatory, discursive, dualistic) thinking. It's a method for breaking our addiction to conceptual thinking. It is a critically important corrective to incessant conceptual thinking; a spiritual practice complements our ordinary utilitarian way of thinking. Because it unifies (especially mind and body as well as self and other) rather than separates, unlike conceptual thinking it has extremely beneficial emotional consequences. Furthermore, just in terms of stress reduction, meditation is healthy.

The Meditative Approach to Philosophy

Meditation is not getting lost in reverie; instead, it involves paying full attention to the present moment. That's a very simple idea in theory, but it's a very difficult one in practice. Nothing less than mastery of living is the goal of meditation. Whereas most of us miss most of our lives because we are elsewhere (thinking about other things, deluded, as if mostly asleep), a meditation master or sage is fully awake, wholly aware of the reality of the present moment (which is where the idea of "enlightenment" or "realization" comes from). How could we possibly be living well if we aren't even fully aware of what we are doing?

Mastery involves something like the kind of absorption that a child has when fully engaged in play—and that joy as well! Someone who lives well is, like a master musician or an athlete in the zone, in a state of continual relaxed concentration in the midst of the incessant hum and buzz of everyday life. Living well is an endless flow experience.

So, it isn't surprising that it requires the same kind of disciplined, intense, persistent practice that also characterizes the training of a master musician or athlete. In fact, it usually (though not necessarily) requires years of the right kind of effort. There are no easy excellences. Since it is so beneficial, everyone who knew about meditation would master it if it were easy. It isn't. Few people ever master it. (Is that surprising? Do most folks ever master anything?) Mastery requires courage, dedication, sustained discipline, and the right kind of training.

Pervasive unsatisfactoriness is caused by separation; it is ended by union. When we act egoistically with separation between ourselves and our acts, we create dissatisfaction for ourselves and others; when we act egolessly without separation between ourselves and our acts, we diminish dissatisfaction. Spiritual practice is the indispensable way to reunion, to living well, to sustained flow experiences.

We all initially try to live better by trying to gain what we like and trying to avoid what we don't like, but this cannot work well. It is false that living better is the process of improving the ratio of positive to negative experiences; rather, **living well is the process of being in the present moment without separation** from any experience.

Nothing is more natural than breathing. Our word 'spiritual' comes from the Latin word 'spiritus', which means 'a breathing.' A spiritual practice is an activity based on awareness of the natural physical process of breathing. Therefore, there is neither anything supernatural or religious about it nor is there anything conceptual about it. It's a deliberate reuniting of mind and body, a healing of mind/body separation.

A spiritual practice is a natural practice. Like 'yoga,' 'meditation' is just another word that denotes a spiritual practic

Zazen

Zazen is the purest kind of meditation.

It's three aims are: to develop concentration, to experience satori-awakening, and to live well by actualizing that awakening throughout all of one's being and activities [enlightenment]. Someone who lives well is said, in honor of the first person we know about who attained it, to have attained "the great Way of Buddha."

Attaining the great Way of Buddha, though, should be a "goalless" goal; once adopted, it should be forgotten!

Instead, remember that the purpose of goals is to enhance the present. Without goals, one tends to drift in the present moment. The task is to become wholly absorbed in living well in the present moment (otherwise, one would be trying to do the impossible, namely, to live well tomorrow today).

In other words, living well is available here and now. Living well cannot occur in either the past or the future. Avoid the mistake of thinking of awakening as something you hope eventually to do someday; like fears and regrets, hopes are usually just distractions, and, instead of nurturing us, egoistic attachments to distractions poison life and prevent us from living (and loving) well. Why make living poorly habitual?

In this introduction it's best to focus only on the first of the three goals, namely, developing concentration. That's all that's required to begin well.

Notice the connection between concentration and feeling good. When you are unhappy, sad, or depressed, you cannot concentrate; you are split from yourself in the sense of engaging in activities (such as eating or walking or washing or working) without paying full attention to what you are doing (because you are distracted or absorbed by your suffering). When you are happy, you are able to concentrate, right? How could zazen possibly work to make you feel better?

It works because it fosters reunion. When you begin to "sit", you'll force yourself to be aware of your breathing. By doing so, you'll reunite your (mental) awareness with your (physical) body. Every time you practice selective concentration by focusing fully on awareness of your breathing, you'll be strengthening your power of concentration by using it (similar to the way that it's possible to strengthen a muscle group by using it regularly with sufficient intensity).

Of course, your ego-I will resist such discipline (just as your body resists serious strength training). **Success requires wholehearted commitment**; nothing less will suffice. As you train yourself over time to practice properly, your power of concentration will improve. As it does, your mind (slowly!) will begin to settle down (imagine sediment settling down in a glass of water once you stop stirring it). This explains why zazen will become the best kind of relaxation possible and why it should be practiced formally once, or, better, twice, daily and informally throughout the day.

A master of meditation is always meditating. As your thoughts settle down, you'll "see" reality more clearly and become less deluded. As that happens, you'll begin to feel better and automatically make better decisions about what to do. If you practice well, in just a few weeks or months you'll be able to tell that you have found a path that is working for you, which will naturally reinforce your practice. That's the way to living well—and there isn't anyone reading these words with understanding who cannot take it and, furthermore, begin to take it today.

If you continue to practice well, eventually more and more frequently you'll become absorbed in whatever you are doing, in other words, you'll be less and less split from your activities. As you teach yourself how to live more deeply in the present moment, you'll naturally become more absorbed in the present moment. As experiences begin more and more to get unstuck and begin to flow, you'll find yourself living "mindfully", which is always better than living forgetfully (which is what you were doing before you started practicing). Though very difficult at first, the more you practice, the easier it gets.

Living mindfully is the result of the long process of extending the kind of fully engaged awareness developed in zazen though all your activities. It's living (as opposed to merely thinking), directly experiencing, the interconnectedness of all individuals. It's living the impermanence and "emptiness" of all individuals. It's experiencing the joy of life beyond cycles of happiness and unhappiness, beyond the reach of conceptual thinking, beyond emotional highs and lows.

Once you learn how to focus fully on your ("little") self or ego-I, it will begin to dissolve like a piece of hard candy in your mouth. When it dissolves, you'll be living well. Why? Since it is your egoistic attachments that are causing you to suffer, to remain stuck, and since all those attachments are based on the self/other distinction, experiencing the dissolution of your self is also experiencing the dissolution of all your attachments—and nothing else is needed to live well! It's not as if you first have to dissolve all your attachments and then do something else; the dissolution of all your attachments will automatically cause liberation!

This is why it is best not to think of living well as an achievement, something you must accomplish or gain; instead, it is more like uncovering something already present, detaching from all sources of sorrow. Though you don't realize it yet, you already are what you need to be to live well. If you do the work to teach yourself how to stop doing what you are now doing, namely, living an incessantly distracted life of egoistic attachments, which depend upon separation and cause suffering, you'll awaken to the reality that you were free all the time without realizing it. (When you stop beating your head against a wall, you'll automatically feel better; there's nothing else required other than stopping what you were doing that was causing the pain.) The sooner you stop living poorly (as a 1 or 2), the sooner you'll begin living well (as a 3).

Change, even when it's an improvement, is always at least uncomfortable. It isn't easy to stop living poorly. Our worst habit, namely, incessant conceptualizing that is rooted in the self/other distinction, is deeply engrained. Though it's simple, it's very difficult to let go of our attachments. Don't worry about it: just keep practicing.

Avoid making excuses for yourself. As an adult, you are completely responsible for what you do, and, if you want, you can immediately begin to do something else. It is not changing that requires time; it is deciding to change that requires time. When you suffer enough, you will either kill yourself or change. Until you actually begin to do what is required (as opposed to merely thinking about it), even exhortations from the Buddha himself would not help you. If you fail to help yourself, you will not live well.

Suppose you are sufficiently sick of suffering to consider actually changing what you do. By itself, changing how you think will not help; it is only **improving what you do** that helps. Are you dissatisfied with your life, with what you are doing? If so, change what you are doing! Only a fool continues to engage in the same kinds of behaviors while expecting different results. If you are hurting and keep doing what you have been doing, you will only keep hurting, and, worse, as time passes, your suffering may intensify. Since you are causing dissatisfaction to yourself and others, why not stop? Why not teach yourself what to do to bring lasting joy to yourself and others?

Suppose you have resolved to do whatever it takes to live well. What should you actually do?

Teach yourself how to sit still. That will help to still your distracted mind.

It's critical to **resolve right now** not to remain stuck just thinking about what to do. Reading good books can help you improve your thinking, but, unless you change what you do, your life will not improve.

———————————

Sidebar quotation from Master Dogen: "Reading sentences while remaining ignorant of how to practice [is like] a student of medicine forgetting how to compound medications. What use is that?"

———————————

If reading or otherwise practicing the method of understanding a bit each day motivates you to practice, by all means read a bit each day; however, if it distracts you from practicing, stop it and get practicing!

The Meditative Approach to Philosophy

A note of caution before beginning to sit: meditation can be a psychological jolt. Occasionally, it can cause, for example, a panic attack. In this sense, it can be dangerous. Since even just starting an effective spiritual practice can be dangerous, the best way to begin is with guidance from a master. There's no substitute for the specific, personal recommendations of a master. Any application of the suggestions in what follows is at the reader's discretion and sole risk.

Like being able to do heavy squats or deadlifts, being able to meditate is a privilege; just as not everyone has the physical ability to do squats or deadlifts, not everyone has the psychological ability to meditate. In particular, some people may require the services of a competent clinical psychologist, psychiatrist, or philosopher before beginning any serious spiritual practice.

In other words, though we all have the ability to practice-enlightenment, some may need professional help before starting effectively. Most people won't have any difficulty.

On the other hand, you might. There's no way to predict in advance. If you do, it doesn't mean that you are unable to meditate. All it means is that you need to get some effective help before you'll be able to begin.

Here's the safety valve: If something scary happens when you are practicing, just let it go and return to your counting. You can always stop meditating, if necessary. Again, it's just a temporary setback.

Sitting Still

Ready to learn how to take your seat? Excellent!

Adopting a good posture is very important. Adopting the right posture enables you as easily as possible to have the right state of mind. There is not, though, just one good posture; there are half a dozen.

If you are flexible enough (and flexibility can be increased), use the fully locked or half locked posture. You are about to learn, though, an easier, more natural posture. It will enable you to start well; following the guidance provided here will help you to begin training yourself, in a correct way, how to still yourself physically. You can learn other postures later.

Environment: Find *a satisfactory place* to sit, and regularly sit there. The closer you can come to making it ideal, the easier your training will go. A quiet room is best. It is best to sit on a mat (or folded blanket) on the floor facing a blank wall. Human voices are the most distracting noises, so at least ensure that you will not have to listen continually to talking, radios, televisions, and so on. Use ear plugs if you need to, or simply get up earlier in the morning when the world is still relatively quiet. Even though one is motionless, "sitting" can generate a lot of heat; for that reason and because it reduces sleepiness, I find a cooler room preferable to a warmer one.

Equipment: It is important to have some padding. Various kinds of pads, cushions, and supports are available from various sources (including the Rochester Zen Center's website). You will need a **mat**: if you do not have a special buttonless one made for meditation, a blanket can be used to make a satisfactory mat; simply fold it into about a 30 inch square and put it on the floor.

If you are interested in a standard mat, try: http://www.endlessknotcushions.com . If you are willing to pay considerably more for a state-of-the-art mat, try: http://www.dharma.net/monstore .

For most positions, you will also need a thick, round cushion (called a **zafu**); this is one piece of equipment you will probably have to purchase because nothing normally available in a home works sufficiently well, though a rolled-up blanket of sufficient thickness or a piece of carpet that is doubled over may serve initially. (If you use the half locked position, it is best to have another cushion to prop up the zafu.)

The Meditative Approach to Philosophy

You do not need a meditation bench if you have a satisfactory zafu; you do not need a zafu if you have a satisfactory bench. You may want to have one of each to alternate during different "rounds" of meditation.

If you are interested in a standard zafu, try: http://www.endlessknotcushions.com. If you are willing to pay considerably more for a state-of the-art zafu, try: http://www.dharma.net/monstore .

You may also want a soft cushion or pillow to support your hands or a cushion to prop up your zafu; they are available from http://www.endlessknotcushions.com .

A **meditation bench** is even easier to use than a zafu. Some inexpensive benches cost about the same as a zafu, but a good bench can cost three times what a zafu costs. On the other hand, a good bench can last you the rest of your life. If you search the internet, you can find different styles. I am extremely happy with my bench, which I purchased from http://www.jameslovegren.com/benches.html .

I recommend using an ordinary inexpensive kitchen **timer**, which will enable you to free your mind from focusing on the duration of your sitting. Decide in advance how long you are going to sit, and set the timer accordingly. The timer should be placed so that you cannot hear it ticking and so that its signal is not too jarring.

How long should you sit? Begin with short periods, perhaps only a minute or so, and deliberately and gradually extend the duration. There is never any reason to sit motionless for more than thirty-five minutes at once. On the other hand, there probably is not much benefit for a beginner to be derived from regularly sitting for less than a total of forty (two twenty-minute rounds) minutes daily (and forty minutes twice daily would be much better).

So, until you work up to that length of time, if you do not expect much benefit from zazen, you will not be disappointed. What counts even more than duration is focus or intensity of concentration [see the next section]. As quickly as possible, extend the duration until you are sitting for at least twenty minutes. Just sit a little bit longer each time, and you'll be there in a few weeks or months.

It is best not to sit with a full stomach; wait at least thirty minutes after a meal. Ensure that you are well hydrated.

Wear dark, loose-fitting clothes; later, if you want, you can buy a robe. (I've purchased more than one robe over the years from http://www.endlessknotcushions.com .)

If you like incense and the place you sit is well ventilated, burn some. The incense I use, which is the best I've ever found, is available from the marketplace section of http://www.rzc.org .

The Meditative Approach to Philosophy

[Incidentally, I have been very pleased with my purchases from these four sources, and I don't receive a kickback for recommending any of them.]

If you happen to have a small bell without a clapper, invite it to sound (to hear the voice of the Buddha encouraging you to come back to your true self!) three times before taking your seat.

Ideally, it is probably best to sit alone sometimes and at other times to sit with a friend or in a group (a sangha). As with physical exercise, having a good partner can be helpful, and having a bad partner can be detrimental; there is nothing wrong with sitting alone.

Sidebar quotation from The Buddha: "If the traveler cannot find / Master or friend to go with him, / Let him travel on alone / Rather than with a fool for company."

Posture: It will probably require some experimentation on your part to find a satisfactory posture. A good posture is one that provides stability, promotes physical immobility, and minimizes muscular tension, pain, and the tendency to fall asleep.

I have helped a number of people find a satisfactory posture, and I have yet to have encountered anyone who was unable at least to get comfortable in the traditional Japanese seiza **posture**. Very briefly, what is most important with respect to any posture is that you **sit erectly** and that you sit **wholly devoid of voluntary movement**.

Here's the posture that is easiest and most natural for nearly everyone. It's a kneeling posture. (If you try it and it doesn't work well for you, simply find another posture that will.)

Set the mat on the floor with its nearest edge a foot or so away from a blank wall. Kneel facing the wall with your knees on the mat near the edge closest to the wall. Your lower legs should be parallel, with knees about shoulder width apart, with the tops of your feet on the mat.

Put the zafu (or rolled up and folded over blanket or piece of carpet) between your ankles and sit back on it; alternatively, you may use a meditation bench. Sit up straight. Adjust the cushion (or blanket) as necessary; increasing its height will decrease the pressure on your knees and the tops of your feet.

Push your belly out to make your back erect and tuck your chin in so that you feel a slight bit of tension in the back of your neck. If you are right handed, put your left hand on top of your right hand with palms facing up and thumbs touching; put your right hand on top if you are left handed. Rest your hands on your lap or on the soft pillow on your lap with their edges touching your abdomen. Gaze down to a spot on the wall a foot or so above the floor; if possible, let your eyes go unfocused. Keep your eyes still. (If you do that successfully, your visual field may darken; if so, that's fine and nothing to worry about.)

Keeping your back erect, relax your shoulders and arms completely. Take a deep chest breath or two, and then just breathe naturally with your abdomen (not your chest). Do not control your rate of respiration. Do not make a technique out of your breathing. Sit motionlessly. That's it!

You should neither be tipped to the left nor to the right; to ensure that you are not out of lateral alignment, you may sit the first time before a mirror stripped to the waist so that you can ensure that the tip of your nose, the tip of your chin, and your navel are in a straight, vertical line. You should neither be leaning forward nor backward. If you do, your back muscles will get sore, which will indicate to you that you were not sitting correctly.

In general, in most standard postures like the one just described, the buttocks and the two knees form a stable base.

Deliberately thrust your buttocks backward and your belly forward so that you slightly tip your hips forward; your lower back should be naturally concave. Swaying left and right once (or a couple of times in decreasing arcs) should help to center your backbone vertically. Pull your shoulders back so that your upper back is directly above the back of your buttocks. Tuck your chin in so the tip of your nose is above your navel. You should feel a lengthening or very slight tension in the back of your neck; this is very important for reducing distracting thoughts. Your teeth should be lightly closed, and your lips should be closed. The tip of your tongue should be on the roof of your mouth just behind your front teeth. Swallow once. Relax your shoulders and let your upper arms hang loosely, naturally close to your sides. Your hands should rest without tension, naturally open, with the right hand supporting the left hand with the tips of your thumbs touching lightly. Look down towards a spot on the wall a foot or so above the floor, but let your eyes go unfocused, which will feel natural after a while. With practice, your center of gravity should shift from high (usually in the shoulders or chest) to low, specifically, to the center of your lower torso, which is a point about two or three inches in from your navel and two or three inches down from there.

Sit motionlessly! Do not, for example, look around, scratch an itch, or readjust your position after you have settled in. To master a stilling meditation, you must teach your body how to remain still! Commit yourself wholeheartedly to enduring minor discomforts without moving for the duration you have selected. However, minor adjustments are permissible. For example, if you find yourself slumping, just push your belly slightly forward and pull your shoulders slightly back.

Even if you are quite flexible and adopt such a good, classical posture, after a while you may begin to feel uncomfortable, and, after even more time, you may begin to feel mild, steady pain or perhaps some numbness in one or both legs. That is normal! There is nothing wrong with you. Instead of moving or focusing on the discomfort or pain, focus with renewed intensity on awareness of your breathing [see the next section]. Because what we focus on expands in importance, the worst procedure would be for you to sit there focusing on your discomfort or pain! Do not worry: you won't get gangrene! Nothing terrible will happen if you sit still for a few more minutes.

Remember: disciplining your body is critical for training your mind, and there's no living well without a trained mind. Of course, if the pain ever becomes severe, such as a throbbing or stabbing pain, end the practice session; however, this almost never occurs.

There is no need to restrict meditation to only formal, measured periods. Since zazen is a nurturing activity, sit whenever you feel that you need nurturing. If you wake up in the middle of the night and cannot go back to sleep because your mind is racing, sit! If you know that some forthcoming event such as an examination or a family gathering will be especially stressful, doing some extra sitting before it occurs may be of great benefit. Furthermore, throughout the day, keep practicing as much as possible; the more you discipline your mind while you are walking or washing or showering or driving or eating or using the toilet or whatever, the more quickly you will free yourself. Someone who lives well does not just live well for one or two brief periods during the day that outweigh suffering all the rest of the time! A sage lives well most the time.

The purpose of stilling the body is to help to still the mind. Now that you understand how to still the body, let's turn toward stilling the mind.

Being Still

If we want to live well, training the mind is critical. Stilling ourselves physically nurtures our ability to still ourselves mentally; physical discipline fosters mental discipline.

If we will train the mind, there's ample peacefulness and abiding joy for everyone.

Sidebar quotation from Yasutani Roshi: "It never occurs to most people to try to control their minds . . . as long as human beings remain slaves to their intellect, fettered and controlled by it, they can well be called sick."

Inattentiveness, the tendency of the mind to get lost in thought trains (sequences of thoughts or judgments), is the dis-ease that naturally afflicts us all.

If you seriously want to liberate yourself and overcome this sickness, this most basic human delusion, you must train the mind. Though it may take years of daily practice to master the art of training (disciplining, stilling, purifying) the mind, in terms of reducing the pervasive dissatisfaction you are causing yourself and others and transforming it into the liberated loving peacefulness of living well, **there is nothing more important to be doing.**

Isn't practicing self-centered? No. The best way for us to be of service to others is to work daily to reduce our own egocentricity, our own self-centered attachments. Healing yourself first is the way to help others heal most effectively.

The best way to begin is to practice being fully aware of our breathing in order to be fully absorbed in the present moment. That is it. It is that simple!

After you have taken your seat, assumed your posture, and settled in, let awareness of your breathing fill your consciousness.

The best **first** practice is counting your inhalations and exhalations. As you inhale, think one; as you exhale, think two; as you inhale again, think three; as you exhale again, think four, and continue in this way until you hit ten and then begin again. If you lose count, do not worry: just go back and begin at one again. That's the first counting practice. That is all there is to it!

Simply by doing that you will be training yourself to be aware of the reality of the present

The Meditative Approach to Philosophy

moment. Be sure not to count automatically, with the back of your mind, while thinking of something else; keep focused on the counting. Pay full attention to each inhalation and exhalation; in particular, let go of thinking about anything before or after the present moment and let go of all thought trains such as stories. If you are thinking of any words other than numbers, you are unfocused. When you can maintain your focus on the counting without getting lost even once for twenty minutes, then you can move on to the **second** counting practice, namely, just counting the exhalations.

When you are able to count exhalations for twenty minutes without getting lost even once, you may go on to a **third** practice, namely, just noticing the inhalations and exhalations. Since this is very difficult, I provide you in The 7 Steps to Mastery with an alternate third practice.[16]

I've just given you what may require months of work. Meanwhile, try to find a suitable teacher. As a third practice, a teacher may assign you a koan (instead of following the breaths).

For the time being, just concentrate on mastering the first practice.

If you are aware of any words other than the counting words 'one,' 'two,' and so on, then you are thinking and not meditating. It can help if you keep a nonverbal image in mind. Please don't get attached to any of them, but here are four suggestions that can help.

(1) Imagine yourself to be a pebble that has plopped into the middle of Lake Superior and you are drifting down, down, down. Let go and let Buddha!

(2) Think of your practice as a drill bit that is boring down into a block of wood to the truth.

(3) Think of your practice like a dog scratching the earth in search of buried treasure.

(4) Think of each exhalation as like the downward swing of an axe or pick and give it all you have.

Don't try to stop extraneous thoughts from arising. When they arise, notice them and simply let them go. Instead of attaching to them, return to focusing fully on counting.

Let your whole attention be directed to disciplining your mind. Instead of holding yourself back (with the intention of protecting yourself), you must hold nothing in reserve. If you are to liberate yourself, you must practice as if your very life depends upon it. I believe it does: **either you'll do it or, in terms of liberating yourself and living well, you'll waste your life.**

Three ingredients are jointly sufficient for success.

The Meditative Approach to Philosophy

First, you must throw yourself wholeheartedly, without reservation, into the practice. This does not mean, of course, that you must throw yourself wholeheartedly into thinking about the practice or its benefits! Let go of thinking in favor of focusing singlemindedly on your breathing.

Second, this must be done with unrelenting effort, with consistency and daily regularity. There is no mastery without persistence.

Third, you must have faith that you can realize your True Nature. With awakening, your need for faith will evaporate.

Sidebar quotation from The Buddha who said that freedom is, or can be, "your greatest joy // Look within / Be still / Free from fear and attachment, / Know the sweet joy of the way."

As well as expecting your body to resist being disciplined, expect the mind to resist being disciplined! It will incessantly provide you with distracting thoughts about what is not real, often something in the past or in the future. That is natural.

When a distracting thought or emotion or bodily feeling or any judgment disturbs your concentration on the awareness of your breathing, please do not get angry and try to force it away, or curse yourself for becoming lost in thought, or get frustrated because you are not already a master meditator.

Instead, be patient with yourself! Be kind to yourself! Be grateful for the reminder that the undisciplined, wandering mind has just given you of how much you really need to increase your control over it, to train it. Notice that distraction and then simply decide to let it pass away of its own accord, much like the reflection of a drifting cloud passes over the surface of a pond, and return to simple awareness of your breathing. **Spiritual training is training in letting go.**

In addition to behaving morally (in other words, with understanding and lovingkindness), it is also critically important to adopt the right attitude. Be grateful that you are able to sit! Be patient and persevering. Be your own best friend! Be light at heart: humor helps. Treat difficulties as opportunities. Be like someone who is enjoying training a puppy or taming an elephant.

The Secret to Success

Meditation is the sword that cuts through knots in the mind. Practice-enlightenment is the way to let life flow.

Meditation is not an escape from reality, an attempt to flee from pervasive dissatisfaction. It is the art of staying calmly focused on what-is in the midst of incessant distractions, the practice of looking deeply into what-is. It's a way of loving dissatisfaction to death. Simply by counting to be fully aware of your breathing during zazen, you are practicing living well. Simply by being fully aware of your bodily activities (such as walking, eating, washing, and working) at other times throughout the day, you are practicing living well, living peacefully.

How could you have peace of mind without practicing being peaceful?

The more you practice well, the better you will live. **Practicing-enlightenment is mastering life.** All your extraneous judgments (dreams, fears, regrets, hopes, remembrances, and so on, which may be 90% of what you think about) are unreal delusions: what is real in the present moment during zazen is your being alive, your breathing. To be real, sit.

Meditation is not conceptualizing (judging, thinking). To meditate is not to think or to believe anything. To meditate is to live (practice, be) a certain way. It is to be wholly centered in the present moment (as opposed to being lost in thought as all those who do not meditate condemn themselves to being). As you sit, your mind will wander away from the present moment and get lost in thought.

The key to practicing well is simply this: **notice that your mind has gotten lost in thought and bring it back to the practice**, the counting of your breaths. Notice and return, notice and return -- thousands of times.

A classic analogy is to training an ox: every time it wanders off course, simply bring it back. Notice that you can train the ox because you are not the ox; similarly, you can train the mind because you are not the mind. A master meditator is free from the otherwise incessant tyranny of thinking; those who do not meditate remain slaves to thinking, which is why they are not free. This explains why meditating is necessary for living well, living freely.

The Meditative Approach to Philosophy

[Incidentally, 'Ironox' is my dharma name. Perhaps my teacher selected it because he thought my mind was as hard and unteachable as iron!]

The practice is pure and simple: enjoy your breathing with no conceptual surd (no intellectual remainder); in other words, the practice is just to be your breathing, your being alive. Eventually, it is just to be your walking or your standing or your working or whatever else you do.

If you patiently sit still and persistently practice bringing the wandering mind back to being fully aware of your breathing and nothing else again and again and again and again and yet again, in a few weeks you will notice that the interval between wanderings is slightly increasing, which will be your first concrete, though subtle, sign that you are on your way to living better. Congratulate yourself for strengthening your ability to concentrate! Understand that you have begun to follow the Way.

If you just keep nurturing yourself, you will soon begin to feel better. For example, within weeks you may notice that you are able to fall asleep more quickly at night and that you sleep more soundly. As distracting thoughts settle down, delusions will have less power over you. Your attachments, including to the idea of accomplishing or gaining something to justify your existence, will diminish.

You may soon want to practice formally for one or two or three or more hours daily. If you keep working well, eventually you will free yourself from bondage of all delusions entirely! You will liberate yourself from slavery, especially from normal slavery to the idea that you are a separate, independent self. As that dissolution occurs, all your attachments will drop away naturally like ripe fruit from a tree, and you will be left with the continual joy of a constant vision of a bare, sparkling reality. **Realization of emptiness permits awareness of fullness.**

There's no reason why you cannot become a master meditator.

One sign of that is that you'll find yourself meditating without realizing that you are meditating.

Will you uncover the truth for yourself? Will you live well? Will you do what is required?

It's wholly up to you. It's your choice. Why not?

Endnotes

1. Rene Descartes, <u>Discourse on the Method for Rightly Conducting One's Reason and for Seeking Truth in the Sciences</u> (Indianapolis, Hackett, 1980; Cress, tr), p. 5.
2. Plato, <u>Meno</u> 80.
3. Rene Descartes, <u>Meditations on First Philosophy</u> (Indianapolis: Hackett, 1979; Cress, tr.), p.17.
4. Plato, <u>Apology</u> 38a.
5. Dennis Bradford, <u>The 7 Steps to Mastery</u> (Las Vegas: Ironox, 2007), section 1.2.
6. I argue in <u>The 7 Steps to Mastery</u> that there is no apprehension of right or wrong.
7. <u>The 7 Steps to Mastery</u>, especially Chapter 7.
8. The <u>Kalama Sutta</u>.
9. <u>The 7 Steps to Mastery</u>, section 3.1, and the section "The Conditioned and the Unconditioned" in my <u>The Three Things the Rest of Us Should Know about ZEN TRAINING </u>(Las Vegas: Ironox, 2007).
10. See <u>The 7 Steps to Mastery</u>, section 11.5.
11. Throughout this section I've relied heavily on Panayot Butchvarov, <u>Skepticism about the External World</u> (N.Y.: Oxford University Press, 1998).
12. Note that, since the particular proposition in question may be contingent, knowledge is not the unthinkability of its falsehood.
13. <u>The 7 Steps to Mastery</u>, section 2.2.
14. <u>The New English Bible</u>, Luke 9: 25.
15. <u>The New English Bible</u>, Luke 9:23.
16. <u>The 7 Steps to Mastery</u>, section 12.5.

If you found the ideas in this book stimulating, I offer many more, for free, on my blog at http://dennis-bradford.com/ . Use the navbar on its left to scroll down to the "Spiritual Well-Being" category and select any posts that might interest you. Please feel free to leave comments or ask questions.

You may find all my books, including a novel, at amazon.com.